OCTOPUSES

by **Elizabeth R. Johnson**

Consultant:
Jody Rake, Member,
Southwest Marine Educators Association

CAPSTONE PRESS
a capstone imprint

Pebble Plus is published by Capstone Press,
1710 Roe Crest Drive, North Mankato, Minnesota 56003
www.mycapstone.com

Library of Congress Cataloging-in-Publication Data
Names: Johnson, Elizabeth R., 1986–author.
Title: Octopuses / by Elizabeth R. Johnson.
Description: North Mankato, Minnesota : Capstone Press, [2017] | Series:
    Pebble plus. Sea life | Audience: Ages 4-8. | Audience: K to grade 3. |
    Includes bibliographical references and index.
Identifiers: LCCN 2015049115 | ISBN 9781515720805 (library binding) | ISBN
    9781515720843 (eBook PDF)
Subjects: LCSH: Octopuses—Juvenile literature.
Classification: LCC QL430.3.O2 J6357 2017 | DDC 594/.56—dc23
LC record available at http://lccn.loc.gov/2015049115

Editorial Credits
Jaclyn Jaycox, editor; Philippa Jenkins, designer;
Svetlana Zhurkin, media researcher; Gene Bentdahl, production specialist

Photo Credits
iStockphoto: richcarey, cover, 13; Minden Pictures: Colin Marshall, 15; Shutterstock: Andrea Izzotti, 9, littlesam, 19, Photonimo, 7, Rich Carey, back cover, 3, 5, 11, 14, 24, Sphinx Wang, 21, Vittorio Bruno, 17

Design Elements by Shutterstock

Note to Parents and Teachers

The Sea Life set supports national science standards related to life science. This book describes and illustrates octopuses. The images support early readers in understanding the text. The repetition of words and phrases helps early readers learn new words. This book also introduces early readers to subject-specific vocabulary words, which are defined in the Glossary section. Early readers may need assistance to read some words and to use the Table of Contents, Glossary, Read More, Internet Sites, and Index sections of the book.

Printed in China.
022016   007718

Table of Contents

Life in the Ocean

An octopus crawls along
the ocean floor. Eight long arms
look for food and places to hide.
Each of its arms can stretch
30 feet (9.1 meters)!

Octopuses live in oceans around the world. Most octopuses like warm water. They live in deep and shallow water.

Up Close

There are more than 300 kinds of octopuses. The smallest octopus is less than 1 inch (2.5 centimeters) long. The biggest is 18 feet (5.5 m) long!

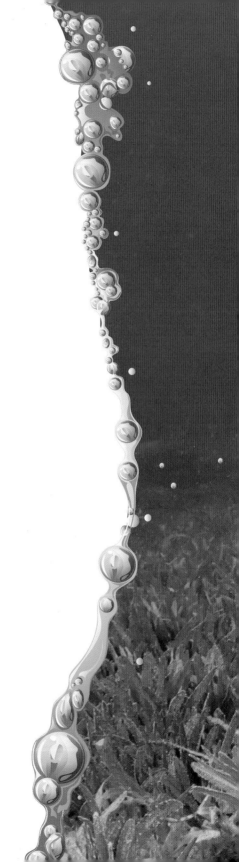

An octopus has a large head.

Its head holds a brain,

a stomach, and three hearts.

Octopuses have no bones. They

can squeeze into tiny spaces.

Finding Food

Octopus arms are lined with
many suckers. Suckers can taste
what they touch. The arms reach
into holes to find food.

With their long arms, octopuses snatch prey. Their sharp beaks and strong tongues can break hard shells. Octopuses eat crabs, lobsters, shrimp, and fish.

Staying Safe

When threatened, octopuses squirt a cloud of ink into the water. The ink confuses a predator. Then the octopus swims away.

Octopuses can camouflage themselves. That means they change color to blend in with their surroundings. Predators have a hard time seeing them!

Life Cycle

A female octopus lays up to 400,000 eggs. Most baby octopuses hatch in four to six weeks. An octopus lives for about one to two years.

Glossary

beak—the horny projecting jaw of animals; the octopus beak looks like a parrot's beak

camouflage—a pattern or color on an animal's skin that helps it blend in with things around it

hatch—to break out of an egg

predator—an animal that hunts other animals for food

prey—an animal hunted by another animal for food

shallow—not deep

snatch—to grab

sucker—a soft, flexible part on an animal's body that is used to cling on to something

surroundings—the things around something or someone

threatened—put in danger

Read More

Olsen, Alana. *Look Out for the Blue-Ringed Octopus! Surprisingly Scary!* New York: PowerKids Press, 2016.

Plattner, Josh. *Octopus: Master of Disguise.* Animal Superpowers. Minneapolis: Abdo Publishing, 2016.

Scott, Janine. *An Ocean of Animals.* Habitats Around the World. Mankato, Minn.: Capstone Press, 2012.

Internet Sites

FactHound offers a safe, fun way to find Internet sites related to this book. All of the sites on FactHound have been researched by our staff.

Here's all you do:

Visit *www.facthound.com*

Type in this code: 9781515720805

Super-cool stuff!

Check out projects, games and lots more at
www.capstonekids.com

Index